A Very Funny Fellow

A Very Funny Fellow

Donald Lev

The New York Quarterly Foundation, Inc.
New York, New York

NYQ Books™ is an imprint of The New York Quarterly Foundation, Inc.

The New York Quarterly Foundation, Inc.
P. O. Box 2015
Old Chelsea Station
New York, NY 10113

www.nyqbooks.org

Copyright © 2012 by Donald Lev

All rights reserved. No part of this book may be used or reproduced in any manner whatsoever without written permission of the author.

First Edition

Set in New Baskerville

Layout and Design by Raymond P. Hammond
Cover Sketch: "Donald in Baseball Cap," oil pastel on paper
©2011 Joanne Pagano Weber

Library of Congress Control Number: 2011942030

ISBN: 978-1-935520-55-9

A Very Funny Fellow

Acknowledgements gratefully accorded the following publications in which poems in this volume first appeared: *Down Under Manhattan Bridge, Caprice, Big Hammer, And Then, Rattapallax, The Saint Ann's Review, Lips, Poetry in Performance, Mudfish, Hudson Valley Poets Fest, The Same, Presa, A Gathering of the Tribes, Chiron Review, New York Quarterly, Automatic Woodstock Anthology, Orbis, Wildflowers, Waterways, Stained Sheets, Polarity, Heliotrope, Chronogram, Half Moon Books Instant Anthology.*

"You're a very funny fellow, but you are no poet."

—Marguerite Harris in a telephone conversation with the author ca. 1971

Contents

I. The Beginnings of a History

THE ACCEPTANCE / *13*
A WINDOW / *14*
IT CAN'T BE ALL LIES / *15*
POLE / *16*
HOMAGE TO THE PLAYWRIGHT / *17*
FAIR BALL / *18*
SAY WHAT IS REAL, MARSYAS / *19*
BIRDSNEST / *20*
BAPTISM / *21*
THE BEGINNINGS OF A HISTORY / *22*
DOG STORY / *23*
RECONNAISSANCE / *24*
FIRE / *25*
THE SERPENT / *26*
LUCK / *27*
THE SPACE THING / *28*
WHAT IT'S ALL FOR / *29*
THE RETURN / *30*
SADDAM HUSSEIN, REQIESCAT / *31*
TO A FRIEND / *32*
EAST OF EDEN / *33*
WHEN I SEEK AN IMAGE / *34*
I BLAME THIS ONE ON THE HEAT AND HUMIDITY, BUT APOLOGIZE ANYWAY / *35*
FEBRUARY 22ND / *36*
DYLAN THOMAS IS THIS POET / *37*
TOTAL ECLIPSE / *38*
GOD IS A RED PEANUT / *39*
GOD'S GIFTS / *40*
THE CREATION OF AMERICA / *41*
ONE SLIP / *42*
IN THIS DREAM... / *43*

THE FESTIVAL / 44
TECHNOLOGY / 45
SO MANY WHO MIGHT UNDERSTAND / 46
DRUNKS / 47
WITNESS / 48
SORROW IS HUMANITY'S COMMON DENOMINATOR / 49
CORPORAL ACTS / 50
CAMPSITE / 51
MY MANTRA / 52
SPECIAL EDITION / 53
I KEPT MISSING / 54
BREAKFAST WITH PRUFROCK / 55
POEM ON A NICE SUNNY AFTERNOON / 56
A PUBLIC RADIO INTERVIEW / 57
SEASONAL POEM / 58

II. A Black Refrigerator

TAKING STOCK / 61
DECEMBER TWENTY-FIRST / 62
LEAP / 63
WHAT YOU PRETEND / 64
THE BUDDHA / 65
CARP / 66
IN THE FOOTHILLS / 67
LINES IN WINTER / 68
THE SECOND DAY OF SPRING / 69
TITANIC / 70
A WIND WAS BLOWING / 71
UNTITLED / 72
A FANTASY OF COMPLIANCE WITH RIGHTEOUSNESS / 73
RELIEF / 74
PASSOVER / 75

ON THE EVE OF EARTH-DAY   /   76
THE LONG AND THE SHORT OF IT   /   77
THE SMALLER TELEVISION   /   78
THE CIVIL WAR: A DOCUMENTARY   /   79
GOTHIC TALE   /   80
TO EMBRACE IT   /   81
A BLACK REFRIGERATOR   /   82
WATERCOLOR   /   83
SIN   /   84
CHALK   /   85
CARNAL KNOWLEDGE   /   86
FAMILY IS EVERYTHING   /   87
THE SACRIFICE   /   88

III. Something Like a Life

NEVER   /   91
MY FATHER   /   92
A MAN AND HIS CLONE   /   93
BOWERY, CIRCA 1950   /   94
STEPPING STONE   /   95
UP-RIVER   /   96
THE END OF THE SERIES   /   97
MEDITATION   /   98
ART-DECO BLUES   /   99
THE QUESTION   /   100
THE MUDDLE   /   101
BRAGGING RIGHTS   /   102
HBO SPECIAL   /   103
CAREER   /   104
BEEFSTEW, TOO   /   105
MY LATEST HOBBY   /   106
LAMENT OF A LESSER PRIMATE   /   107
THIS BIG WINDOW   /   108

I. The Beginnings of a History

THE ACCEPTANCE

My pains did not cease until after midnight. I don't know what took the analgesic so long to work, but relief did come and I fell asleep.

I did not dream so much as guess at life—clutch at forms that vanished in my hands. The sky, not necessarily above, but more beside, was filled with bells. These would not ring so long as I would not hear them.

I awoke full of the usual apprehension. The pain of being did not set in right away.

I have made it a habit to stop in the little donut shop every morning to read my paper and consume the breakfast special. The waitress brings me my usual with great efficiency, even haste, but often does not get around to my coffee refill before feelings of exasperation begin to arise in me. Once the second cup is downed, however,

well-being begins to rise and swell in me and I can proceed to face the day with resignation if not resolution.

The token was inserted by me into the appropriate slot. I heard the mechanism's acceptance, and felt satisfied that something in this world fitted.

A WINDOW

A window you can't see out of or into:
I sit before it like a cat,
Contemplating what?
There are other places, I suppose—
Other points of view.
But just this one holds my interest.

IT CAN'T BE ALL LIES

It can't be all lies.
Surely some of it
Could pass the test.
We all go down to that
Deep puddle off Main Street
And see who can hold his
Best friend's head under longest.
That should prove something.
Are there any questions
Or answers?
Any requests?
It must be time for lunch.
Then maybe a long run
Away from the dogs.
And then back to the symposium.
The panel on perplexity should be
Interesting. That on suicide
A must.

POLE

Hands surround a pole, a left above a right.
The pole is for defense, perhaps.
But maybe it's for vaulting or fishing.
See here, it could certainly be used for aggression!
Or maybe it's just to reach up to that tree
To get the little boy's cap down for him
From the branch where the big boys had flung it.

HOMAGE TO THE PLAYWRIGHT

"Click," says Brick (played by Paul Newman). "Click. I'm waiting for the click." Here we sit in a darkened theater, the theater of our darkened imagination, waiting for a click that will bring us ice cold water from the deepest well of being. We will use this as a chaser only. But we must find a liquor worthy of it.

        I can't read what I have written here. The theater is too dark. Well, I do not wish to look now. There'll be time to look later. I suspect I have written trash. The darkened imagination, though. That is a fearful image! A theater full of folks awaiting sudden illumination. Let's move them quietly toward the exit.

FAIR BALL

Fair Ball. Hit into the beautiful blue sky then
falling into play.
In the stands are crowds of onlookers drawn
from sweetest imagination.
As the third baseman scoops the ball up and

speeds it to its destination—
the peanuts in the air, the lager, the boiling franks—
where can I go with this?

SAY WHAT IS REAL, MARSYAS

with apologies to Iris Murdoch and Barbara A. Holland

Say what is real, Marsyas
Or is it all literature?
Good chicken soup with matzohball from genuine Jewish take out place
a rarity in America, you know. Even in Brighton Beach
not so common anymore.
But the taste, Marsyas
is something to get flayed alive for.
Well that is an exaggeration, but
you know what I mean.

BIRDSNEST

A birdsnest—a rather large one—
as precise an observation as I am capable of—
has been lying on the ground in front of my house
all winter, and has just become visible as the snow has been melting.

Perhaps I should, haiku like, leave it at that.

A flawed symbol of spring.

BAPTISM

I just slid under
waters prepared from the beginning
for me. For only me.
There are treasures hidden at the bottom
if only I could ever reach it.
I slid under yet here I am
shaking the wet out
and spilling something on the page
that again misses the point.

THE BEGINNINGS OF A HISTORY

This Siberian tiger
who would not consent to be extinct
looked down off his hunk of ice
and surveyed the crowd of tourists and
ground floor entrepreneurs.
He was searching for a friendly face
but finding only masks.
Ivanovich, an old
retired party hack, who gratefully remembered
the good old days and how he survived them,
stepped forward. He smiled from ear to ear and
uttered an old political joke only he and the tiger understood.
You can imagine how tired everyone else was of waiting
for what, nobody knew.

DOG STORY

A beautiful old dog, meandering on the highway.
Cars mercifully stop to let him get out of their path.
He is searching for someone or something;
who or what maybe he isn't sure he remembers.
He attempted to follow me, I don't know why,
up my old wooden stairs, where my cat would be
sure to greet him warmly.
How was I responsible? Yet I was sure I was.
I sort of led him back to his own domain.
He belonged somewhere up a dead-end road
but everyone was gone this quiet Sunday afternoon.
When I got back to my own side of the road I
turned and saw someone who obviously knew him
take him in hand. Not everything ends up so well.

RECONNAISSANCE

I'm just going to sit here in my car,
in this little shopping center in Villeville, New Jersey,
and look at the moon   the stars   the night   the nothingness,
the All, the All-in-All,
the concrete, the treated lawn,
the bank   pizza restaurant   Dunkin' Donuts   A&P.
Armies are we,
advancing under orders we'll never see.

FIRE

I didn't cry fire in a crowded theater.
First of all, the theater wasn't crowded.
And I didn't cry fire or cry anything at all.
I probably merely murmured.
See I was watching this film about Adolf Hitler—
his last days in the bunker with Eva and his
typical dumb but pretty forties style secretary
(they don't make them like that anymore,
thanks to the women's movement).
Well they were all truly great actors,
the best I suppose Germany has to offer,
particularly the guy who played Hitler.
Wow. What a job. He managed to
get across both the historic monster and
the kind of sweet side (Hitler was, after all,
a politician, and a boss a "Munich girl"
couldn't help but have a crush on).
And then there was Goebbels und der missus and
killing, oh so tenderly all their children—
the idealism really comes across, no
doubt about it. End of any idealism for me. If
any was left at my advanced age.
Ok. I was supposed to respond with
understanding? With sympathy?
What happened was I came to realize just how strong the concept
"enemy" is. These were fucking Enemies.
I've been living alone quite a while now and
I suppose I talk to myself and I
might have murmured something
in the theater. All of a sudden
it's a crime to respond to a movie you're watching?
What the fuck's been happening?
That wasn't the way it was when movies were
movies, back in New York City anyway.
So some scumbag in the row in front of me shushes me.
Well fuck him. And fuck Hitler too!

THE SERPENT

The serpent—did you actually speak to it?
Did you get it to lead you down into its hole,
show you the family drawings on the sides of its
lair—the writings of its ancestors in proto-Sanskrit—
shake its rattle at you and sing you its
love songs and its death songs?
And if all that transpired, how has it affected you—
your diabetes, for instance—or your insatiable hunger for
young boys...?

LUCK

Like manna from Heaven
luck poured down on me.
I didn't know which way to turn.
That's tragic, isn't it?
The manna kept falling
on my shoes, in front of me
and behind me...
I'm a lucky man,
for what it's worth…

THE SPACE THING

What about space?
What about it?
There's so little of it.
What?
I mean for me here.
Oh, well.
I'd fall over myself, but there's no room to fall.
Try deep breathing. Meditation. Stuff like that.
I'm trying it now.
Any success?
My limbs are all twisted
and I have a headache where my third eye should be.

And you know that space thing?
It still makes me angry.

WHAT IT'S ALL FOR

The ice cap is melting
explains
the patient
scientist
to the schoolchild
on public radio
Which means America
east of Niagara Falls
will be under water

This house, on a hill,
as well as our family's graves on Long Island
  will be
  on the bottom of the sea.

So what's it all for?
asks
the unanswerable
  Cynic

THE RETURN

for Ira Cohen

All sounds stopped. The instruments muted.
If birds there were, they were unheard.
And every soul sat cross-legged on the ground
intoning eternal ohm to energize
ailing poet, home at last from his travels,
head bowed under his large hat
like sleeping mexican under sombrero
on my mother's cookie jar.

SADDAM HUSSEIN, REQIESCAT

Obviously
friendless,
pulled out of
a hole
like a beet
or potato,
and hanged—

      not shot—

that,
      his ghost
will always
      remember.

TO A FRIEND

Sunshine, blue skies, suddenly
darken. People are like that too.
God I didn't think I'd be so moved
when the sunshine of your visage turned that blue
I mean prune blue tearstained blue
I know what pain is. That's all I can legitimately say to you.

EAST OF EDEN

I don't live in the neighborhood.
Sorry.
I'm lost too.
I wandered down this rather boring main street,
then I turned up one street
and down another.
Which I shouldn't have done, with my
notorious lack of a sense of direction.
Now I am somewhere, I guess.
It looks like most other places.
Any town or any city.
A McDonalds a Burger King a
Rite Aid drug store.
The street's pretty wide and it's called Washington Street.
There is a traffic light, and several cars going each direction, so
I guess it is a large town or a city.
I begin to wonder what I thought I was doing here.
Then I just thought how my feet hurt.
It will be daylight soon.
I hope I can avoid the quicksand.

WHEN I SEEK AN IMAGE

When I seek an image of all I have
lost, been exiled from in my
sixty-seven years I only conjure up a
fragment of an impressionist painting
of a street partially bathed in sunlight.
There are stores and fruit stands but I
have to find somewhere to hide for
this scene is both familiar and very
strange. I look for a place, a public
park perhaps to loiter in, a street I
can walk disconsolately in. This is
nowhere I've been. This is
everywhere I've been. This is past
present and future all together.
Maybe I'll cross over to that field on
which is being played some game. I'll
watch a while then look for a library
or a tavern, a diner or a funeral parlor
to rest in; an all-night movie theater or
a cheap hotel. Now I'm back too far.
I'm losing my audience. Instead I'll
find my car, drive out of town, put in
at a shadowy motel, take a shower,
watch tv, score some drugs to
maybe o-d on.

I think I've blown the image—through
lack of discipline. Let's return there.
Recognize a corner drugstore. Or a
railroad trestle beautifully
architectured in fog. I begin to make
out figures in the street, young men,
young women. But forty years have
obliterated any chance of recognition.

Exile is fantasy. The past never was.
All that ever was for me is here,
sitting in my chair, seeking images.

I BLAME THIS ONE ON THE HEAT AND HUMIDITY, BUT APOLOGIZE ANYWAY

I walked along this stream, fish kept biting my feet.
But it was cool and stony and I was
involved with nature.

These birds suddenly flew up into a branch of
a tree just above my head.
There was something strange about them.
They were red feathered wide eyed and had these
really bad teeth sticking out of their beaks which made them
look silly even for birds.
They eyed me in a funny way and seemed to be laughing.
I just stood in the water and was miffed.
This wasn't what I expected from all those nature films I
watched on the nature channel or reading National
Geographic.

I looked around for a canoe to hail, but it started raining,
and you know how hard it is to hail a canoe when it's raining.
Now I began to realize what a pickle I was in. I got out my
cell phone, thank god I had a cell phone, and called my office for help.
I did have an office, thank god, an office and a cell phone, otherwise
I would really find myself with a problem I could not solve.

Well, thank god I survived the wilds.

I don't know what else to say on this subject, except
that I should probably choose a different subject next time I write.

FEBRUARY 22ND

Today is the birthday of
the father of my country
and the mother of
I guess my unique personality.

They weren't pleasant people either of them.
George had those painful plates in his mouth.
My mother had a mouth.

But George refused a crown
and limited himself to two terms.
These were gifts that permitted whatever
democracy we have now.

And my mother had an eye for the truth.
And the words to batter me with it.

DYLAN THOMAS IS THIS POET

"Dylan Thomas is this poet," my friend Charlie Barton
told me (God, was it fifty years ago?), "who just got stinking
drunk and wrote this great poetry."
That's for me, I thought.
Long afterwards I discovered
Thomas only wrote when sober, two lines at a sitting,
mostly hung over, then raced for his eye opener as soon
as the pubs opened.
But the first myth was enough. I found my calling.
And here I am. Never tried the two perfect line
method, but
I've used others.
Happy New Year. It's January what? Third?
And I'm still drunk. You know? I might just try
Dylan Thomas' approach. Consider that my
New Year's resolution. L'chaim!

TOTAL ECLIPSE

Tonight I stood outside a bar in New Paltz,
with a young man celebrating his 33rd birthday

by getting soused on pitchers of beer
and setting his beard on fire.

We watched the shadow of the earth
pass over the face of the moon.

A third of the way
through I said good-bye,

and wished my friend safe journey
through his crucifixion year.

GOD IS A RED PEANUT

for Charlie Barton, wherever he is

"God is a red peanut"
uttered humorously by my "black protestant" atheist
friend Charlie long ago; I do not remember
whether before or after he had flung my newly
acquired crucifix to the floor—
But I just heard at a poetry reading—I,
awkwardly, do not remember the
identity of either the poet or the poem—
that the Aztecs saw God imbedded in a pea,
and could not conceive of the notion of a
God Who is everywhere.
And at once I was overwhelmed with
the understanding of just how devout
a believer was my black protestant atheist friend!

GOD'S GIFTS

God gave us all
our tasks to do.
Like the dung beetle
(as I've only just learned)
who follows monkeys around
    & eats their dung.
Me, he gave all that
    taxi driving—
        and dishwashing—
to do;
which I resented until now!

THE CREATION OF AMERICA

Sitting watching fireflies under starry skies
thinking of William Jennings Bryan dying
after his defense of God against
the monkey worshipping atheists.
Dayton, Tennessee.
They say now it was a gimmick to lure
tourists to the poor little town.
Scopes was a gym teacher subbing
at biology and put up to it by the town
fathers.

Is it always the sincere who lose
at any game?

I ask the fireflies, the stars, the
Great Spirit who the chief Tecumseh
thought would vanquish the sickly whites…

Clarence Darrow was sincere as well; the outcome
of the debate is still in doubt.

ONE SLIP

One slip. One fall, even if it's just to one's knees is all it takes to be counted out. A tough game. What am I doing here? It has something to do with what I hold in my arms. A babe, a lantern, a woman, a bag of groceries, a pile of books? I'm slipping. Maybe I'll cash in some bottles and cans, major commerce in my world—capitalism on the march!

–Rego Park. One town over. Don't mix up 63rd Street and 63rd Drive, not in Queens. It's the only advice I can give anyone about anything. Oh can you see how bravely the stars are shining? The Milky Way is eating up the rest of the cosmos just like us. First Flushing then Kew Gardens then Jamaica. I'll try to head west again. Anything to escape my origins. It is after sundown. Yom Kippur. And here I am eating a ham sandwich. Will I never grow up? I want to rush into the arms of the Eternal, say here I am. I have been seeking Thee with my whole heart all of my life, here I am. I want to cling like a babe to the source of life and not feel silly. No. I want to be silly without feeling I am ignoring other worlds. Without end. Amen. I see a priest bow his head toward the elevated host and I want that priest to be me. I want to feel free to touch the Torah scroll. I want to find some niche in the human family. I want to root for the Yankees or the Twins. All I can do now is chew on a ham sandwich, swig beer, and entertain very fleeting thoughts…

IN THIS DREAM...

the computer
threatened
to set itself afire.
My ineptitude was driving it crazy.
I questioned it too much!
Oh God of Israel
are you that hypersensitive?
If so I am lost.

THE FESTIVAL

All of them...
well not all of them but
all who were in town
were under that stupid roof open to the
scatological skies;
all digging deeply
into themselves
with tablespoons to hold the pain precisely.

That is our national literature.
Not all of it, naturally, but enough of it.

TECHNOLOGY

What a funny contraption. There's a
place to put nine of your ten fingers, but
no place for your toes. Or your nose.

I'll have to refresh my memory on how to use it, or try to
find the instructions, which I discarded in a sudden fit of
despair.

I know the world is waiting for me to
rise to the next level, and it pains me
to keep it waiting.

SO MANY WHO MIGHT UNDERSTAND

So many who might understand me
will never read this poem.
They would have understood my longing
to have all those intricate familiar relationships
with parents, grandparents, siblings, progeny
all sharing memories of decent, but maybe
falling apart houses, neighborhoods changed
almost beyond recognition, signals retrieved, signals
ignored, signals betrayed...
But this is not me. I have no language to
explain myself, so that Garrison Keillor's

soft voice might recite *my* poem, gently nudging the insights,
and have all of Public Radio America say, "oh yes..."

DRUNKS

Drunks are always meditating
on universal structures
which deny them
the fluidity they deserve.
Drunks are always meditating,
occasionally viewing
in behind-bar mirrors
buddhas
that do not console, but ask…
Drunks are always meditating
on the protective shell around them.
How brittle it is.

WITNESS

I just witnessed
via barroom television
a massive barbecuing
I mean one that went on and on
Americans from every region
chewing up that pig meat
and guys with smocks and
baseball hats turning sizzling
slices of meat with various implements
and one scene had doomed porkers themselves
made to race like horses or dogs!
Now that should've been ok. God knows I
eat meat! My father, from a family of butchers,
liked his well done; I understand cowboys share
that sentiment. But I eat meat.
Why then did I have to watch
this murderous orgy through the eyes of
a vegetarian? What O Spirit of Righteousness
art thou trying to say to me?
That my species, *homo sapiens*, is the most
vicious, most disgusting in the universe?
I sincerely hope not!

SORROW IS HUMANITY'S COMMON DENOMINATOR

The bully has sorrow.
The victim has sorrow.
The dictator has sorrow.
The democrat has sorrow.
Hitler, Goebbels, and Himmler, believe it or not, had sorrow;
as did Anne Frank
as did Edith Stein
as did your grandparents.
Your mother had sorrow.
Your father had sorrow.
Your sister, your brother, your aunts & your uncles
all have or had sorrow.
Stalin had sorrow.
Pol Pot had sorrow.
Saddam Hussein must have had sorrow.
Maybe even Ronald Reagan had sorrow.
Maybe even George W. Bush has sorrow.
After all, everyone else does.

CORPORAL ACTS

I am grateful for people
the meaning of whose lives
lie in caring for others

But I, I
am more the anti-hero type,
the Dostoevskian undergrounder
full of sores, angers, and perversions

bellowing against everything!

Thank God for those others!

CAMPSITE

Here it is. Here is where we set up camp.
Around us the forest, the stark craggy mountains,
the fast rushing streams,
and the animals of our lives.
We shall pause, once we have lit the fire.
We shall contemplate all that is despicable.
We shall plant our eyes on the eyes of liars.
We shall breathe deeply within the pure air
the stench of those who trade on misfortune,
who carry everything they touch back to their own filthy
lairs…

MY MANTRA

First I tried listening to my own breaths.
Then I tried counting them.
I crossed my legs and
let my third eye stare into space,
but for all my trouble
I did no better
than find myself
being driven wildly around Hollywood
in a taxicab.

Peter Falk was on my left holding my hand
while on my right
sat Cary Grant
pouring me a shot of gin from a silver flask.
No one was in the driver's seat.
Let me out, I cried continually.
Which was exactly
my mantra.

The cab stopped. The door opened.
And I stepped out
onto a cloud.

Let me out, I cried.
It was, after all, my mantra.

SPECIAL EDITION

...yes the stones
abounding in a field or
bit of beach
so many the rain rains on, the
waves rush in and out on
like so many little literary magazines
each such a distinct and special creation, really.
Listen to the thunder, or the
ocean if you're near to it,
& contemplate your own dear little life!

I KEPT MISSING

I kept missing this little road I was to turn down on.
I would go past, turn around
and overshoot it again and again

but I finally got to the place
which was a temple dedicated to the gods
I should have been worshipping
when instead I was turning aside
looking at things not particularly holy.

I have waited for the thunder and lightning
to subside, the heavens to relax their anger
before I embarked on this,

which is the poem
so real it scratches.

BREAKFAST WITH PRUFROCK

A small black ball replaced the
peach I no longer dared not eat.
I didn't know it would be that
impatient with me.

I had rolled up my jeans carefully that day
and carefully teased out of its box a mound
of shredded wheat. Then at last went for the peach.

A metaphor for my life, I thought! But that's as far as I got.

POEM ON A NICE SUNNY AFTERNOON

We all have or pretend, like me, we have
a friend or neighbor like this:
who invited me next door to his
parents' and forbears' stately mansion,
where the swimming pool was just
filled with vodka!

I said yes indeed I will come along, just
let me get my bathing suit and...
I'm not at all sure of what I added, but
I cut through the jungle underbrush to
reach this place from mine, and
dived into a pool of vodka!
(excuse the exclamation points, but really!)
I swam around in it, it was so nice and cool and
refreshing, and some of the more
athletic bathers were tossing olives and
onions around in it. I want
to go somewhere with this...
to make it, you know, worthwhile...
I believe I became a poet for the most
worthy reasons...but now...I just don't know...

A PUBLIC RADIO INTERVIEW

Eighty eight years young and he's still shoveling shit.
I say, Mr. L. What's it like to be eighty eight and still shoveling shit?
Well, if you asked me if I was eighty eight years old and not shoveling shit,
I would have an answer that it would be awful.
But as it is, being eighty eight or whatever and shoveling shit is for me
the only imaginable way to live. I've been doing it since I was
13, and if I do say so myself, I am very good at it.
Well, you certainly must know all the ins and outs of shit shoveling.
You must be privy to any number of trade secrets.
Well, there is a right way and a wrong way of shoveling shit.
You must get the right amount on your shovel if you don't want to shovel it
all over your shoes. And then you must be able to gauge the consistency
at any one time, be aware of the seasons the weather. Winter shit
for instance, is often frozen. Then you have very wet shit
when it rains. All must be handled accordingly.
Do you think you'll retire soon, now that you're eighty eight?
What would I be retiring to? What would I do if I wasn't shoveling shit?
Thank you for speaking with us, Mr. L. And happy birthday!

SEASONAL POEM

A bitter winter. I might say a long bitter winter
but we still count only the three conventional months
between solstice and equinox as winter and are
not halfway between at the moment.

May we look forward to a long sweet spring,
a long hot summer, and a long poignant fall,
and another long, bitter winter, those of us
lucky enough.

II. A Black Refrigerator

TAKING STOCK

It isn't snowing yet.
I cancelled out of a
poetry reading in Woodstock
because I was afraid to drive
home in what was threatening to be
a snowstorm.

I am ashamed of myself.

The last poem I wrote, "Blandsville,"
was about my origins in Forest Hills Queens
and ended with 3-year-old me sitting in a playground,
experiencing exile.

Shame and Exile. I continue to write
what a good friend of mine, not in an unkind way, called
"your depressing little poems"…

though "Blandsville" was a bit longer than most of my poems.

DECEMBER TWENTY-FIRST

Around we go again hooray!
The longest night has
passed for this year,
and now the days are to become longer.
Paul Winter has once more
commanded the sound of my radio
from the great unfinished cathedral
in Manhattan
and oh how many voices cry
tearfully for peace this year as
every year
and how many others
stand their ground and growl.

LEAP

Mountain peak.
Cloud surrounded.
Has she skied down to where I wait with
a brandy cocktail and a cigarette?
German tanks are poised
at the edge of the property
and I pour another drink.

Edith Piaf is singing something
soulful in the background
as I eye the skies.

Marlene Dietrich watches all with her dark eyes.

I wake in a future, surprised.

WHAT YOU PRETEND

It's what you pretend to do.
Sit in the whirling bath of life
like a clay statue
then at some later time take a sharp instrument
to the clay tablet
the gods have made of your voice
and jump down with it
and talk to somebody, anybody.
See if they hear something you say. See if
they laugh somewhere near where you laugh
as if it's ok
that you
you know…

THE BUDDHA

The Buddha visited me today.
He was on my porch knocking on my door
as I came down to breakfast.
I recognized him as an old friend I
understood to be living in Connecticut these many years
and not having any reason
to communicate, his having taught me all I could absorb.
Yet here he was, so I invited him in.
I offered him tea or wine. He chose nothing.
I had a plumbing problem he took care of for me
and something with my computer he also remedied.
Then he left. We'd barely spoke.

CARP

Thinking about those big carp
swimming up the Mississippi
preparing to invade the Great Lakes…
What a triumph!
I am picturing carp, broiled
or boiled in the big dairy
restaurant in Brighton Beach
in tomato sauce I picture it;
and the Russian groceries
would let you buy live
carp to swim in your bathtub
till you were ready to feast—
and the feature at Chinese restaurants:
whole golden carp—
sounding like the notes of a hymn or carol.
What nerve these sallow mid-west Americans
have to oppose the progress
of the holy missionary carp into their
native waters.
What nerve!

IN THE FOOTHILLS

Wine is a part of it.

The riddle of missing fingers.

I can still grasp
a tall staff
and plod my way
across lowlands
to the foothills of high mountains;
where I must stop
to catch my breath
before continuing or returning.

I am at such a stopping place now.
I have been here a long time.
I shall probably be here a while longer.

I shall not hesitate to communicate
what little there is to communicate.

LINES IN WINTER

for Enid

Snowflakes cling to the yew hedge
furnished by a cemetery's
program for perpetual care.

Many miles away I watch
snow gather
upon denuded rose of sharon bushes
outside my window.

A shadow
passed behind me
just now. I felt it.

Something's vanished.
Nothing has taken its place.

THE SECOND DAY OF SPRING

This little bird—I
suppose he's little, I
have never actually seen him—
but here he is chirping
nonstop his boring song.
He does so every spring.
The world is warmer now
and beginning to fill with
minimalist music.
I have to find something
to do with my brain.
Tomorrow it will rain.
I'll write that letter
I've been meaning to write
to Mallarmé—asking him
just what the dead *can* know
of oblivion.

TITANIC

I can't stop to write this now.
I am sliding down the deck
of a luxury liner that is listing.
Soon I will be crashing headlong into the sea.
My love has already preceded me.
All around is utter chaos.
The lifeboats have all been let loose
and the crew is maintaining order
by shooting the more panicked
among the remaining passengers.
So you see why I cannot write this just now;
till I have had a chance to recollect it in tranquility.

A WIND WAS BLOWING

A wind was blowing.
Stuff was being blown around our heads. I bent to my work
trying to make sense of the storm.

I got thrown onto this veranda,
landing on a
little bed with nice quilting. I heard footsteps I hoped was
but nope. It wasn't.
What I am doing making note of all this, I
do not know.
But I am planning to compile everything into a book
I shall call "Notes."

UNTITLED

The world ended the day before yesterday.
Everyone was taken up in a Universalist rapture except me.
I had a reading scheduled for today.

A FANTASY OF COMPLIANCE WITH RIGHTEOUSNESS

OK here I am
stumbling around in the mud
with these rusty clippers
trying to cut these tendrils
sprouted aimlessly about by
an invasive species hell bent to strangle to death my
late wife's beloved rose of sharon bushes.
I had been ordered into this action
by a neighbor of mine, Charles,
who caught me moving my car a yard or two from the
vicinity of the bank
to a place closer to the drug store
in order to save a few steps.
He was outraged, as I should have been,
by my gross disdain of exercise.
So here I am snipping away at this
impregnable canopy of branches
attempting an interference with nature
that is indeed a violation of my own nature
as a rotten bag of lazybones quite content to be so.

RELIEF

This leg stuck out of the closet
where the door was ajar.
I was careful not to trip over it.
I am cautious by nature.
I felt a lot of relief that I
didn't need anything out of that
closet at such an obviously inopportune moment.
I still feel a sense of relief, which
I suspect is something permanent.

PASSOVER

After the seder we met, Bergman and I,
for a game of chess by the sea.
He looked unusually pale,
but very sure of himself.
I claimed too great a deficiency in chess
to compete so seriously.
He eyed me wearily, as though
he'd heard that excuse so
many times before...
We listened in silence while the
sound of timbrels accompanied
the rest of the celebrants
filing over the hill past us.
Then we played till daylight erased us.

ON THE EVE OF EARTH-DAY

As locusts fell on Australia
and Icelandic volcanic ash
fell on western Europe
I stood on Highway 375
approaching Woodstock
surrounded by smoke emanating
from under the hood of my stubbornly
inert Ford Taurus.

Such is the world and in some
obscure way,
I am grateful to be part of it.

THE LONG AND THE SHORT OF IT

Everyone at the front of the bar was
drunker than I had ever seen anybody
but they all stood drinking beers with
shots of that German stuff everybody drinks now.
One of the guys, who I think owned the place, though
he seemed too young to own a bar, but
maybe that was because most bar owners in my
long memory had been infinitely older than I was.
I guess those days are over. Anyhow
the generous guy buying the drinks included me in.
And they had pizza they were sharing
round the bar and I got two slices even though
I didn't know anybody very well.
One guy was going on how he was 33
the same age Jesus was, you know,
and I assured him that most of us
survive that thirtythird year and
never look back.
I asked the owner if it was somebody's
birthday and he told me
his best friend was dying today
and he'd get the phone call when he
got home.

All I could say was "oh."

THE SMALLER TELEVISION

The smaller television near the front of the bar
and comfortably within the scope of my
better left eye, showed tigers
running down gazelles, then lions
sneaking up on elks—
and so on—a parade of carnivores
consuming vegetarians.
My vision dropped on down
to the engraving of George Washington
lying beside my beer;
then, evading nature and
skipping history,
my mind returned to its lair.

THE CIVIL WAR: A DOCUMENTARY

That string music
will get you every time.
Even if the voice-overs, the gravelly voiced actors
intoning immortal words of generals and presidents, even
poets, don't—
and of course the black and white visions of horrors
in fields, in hospitals, the maimed, the murdered crying out
for
lack of anaesthetics—

and you wonder why you're not understanding.

It continues.

All the art thrown against it. It continues.

GOTHIC TALE

Golden sunlight was passing over
the little green field
with the lovely flowers
and the graves of
murdered parents.
A rabbit hopped onto one of the gravestones
and sat there a few seconds before bounding off.
My sister and I searched the sky for rainclouds
which we did not find.
Anything would have brought relief.
But a sour note sounded in the distance
from a soulless trumpeter.
And we began to weep like children
who were, after all, not to be punished.

TO EMBRACE IT

Rattattattattattattattattat this old guy with mustaches
down past his adam's apple
he is the friend and mentor of our hero, well he's
killed his share of other guys but he
catches one himself. Poignant.
The hero, as I guess he is, he's killed more
than anybody but I guess they're the bad guys—
I don't know how you can tell the bad
guys from the good guys until the
hero shoots one, and there's one
gorgeous female in this and she's
armed too rattattattatatt and she
kills her share and ends the film bleeding
to death in the arms of our hero
and I find it pretty sickening and
remember why I elected to
pass such films by when they came
to my neighborhood movie theater. But I've been buying up
these cheap videos to kind of review
the past...But reality just can't be like this.
But then news comes in fom say Somalia or Kyrgyzstan
and I think of Martin Buber's saying that
the world is incomprehensible, but
embraceable, and I try my damnedest
to embrace it.

A BLACK REFRIGERATOR

I should never have bought a black refrigerator.
The men who delivered it left a screendoor open
and my little black cat Kit Smart took the opportunity
to take off. He needed to go to the vet.
I think he just looked for a cool spot in the woods to die in.
Meanwhile Tuli Kupferberg and Harvey Pekar died.
And a big bomb exploded in Uganda killing lots of people.
The point is, never buy a black refrigerator.

WATERCOLOR

I named the sailboat "Enola Gay"
contemplating graceful progress
across gentle waters,
like that ship across those
skies that perfect day…

SIN

There was this rule:
thou shalt not piss
upon the Tree of Life.
But I had to go.
The next gas station
wouldn't be for another
thirty-five miles and I
just couldn't hold it any longer.
So I pulled off the road and
went behind this tree.
How could I have known
it was *that* tree. And I
never heard of that particular
rule. Maybe I wasn't listening or
something. I shouldn't feel guilty,
should I? Should I?
The Tree of Life just shriveled
up and died. How could I have known?

CHALK

Chalk it up to climate change if you want,
but the ghosts are really crawling out of the woodwork this
breezy October. The ghost of Joseph Stalin, for instance,
materialized singing. I asked him whether he was regretting
all the damage he did in life. "Blame it on my wife," he retorted,
"her and her vindictive Jewish relatives! I see you've got my picture
on your wall." "I bought it in Brighton Beach," I told him.
"It's sort of a joke."
"I don't get the joke," he said,
and disappeared.

CARNAL KNOWLEDGE

I watch you through my sincere blue eyes
take off your brassiere
and my mind suddenly races like clouds in a windy blue sky
and I see our children signing papers
to allow us into a nursing home...
How beautiful...how beautiful you are...

FAMILY IS EVERYTHING

Did anyone call? No?
Just someone wanting to
fit me up with cable.
Maybe I should. No I shouldn't.
Television's worse than loneliness.

Family. Family is everything.
Someone in an old movie said that.
I remember rooms full of family
everyone talking at once, mostly
in a language I didn't understand.

Wonder where they've all gone to.
No I don't. I guess most of them multiplied
and populated the earth. I'll find one of them someday
say, hey, cousin! My cousin will probably just
shrug his or her shoulders and move on.
It's what I'd do.

Maybe I should get cable.
It'd serve me right.

THE SACRIFICE

The weather turned damp and chilly
and I have a cough and a wheeze.
I climb these slippery wooden stairs up to my door
pushing a bag of groceries and a box of wine
before me. I climb as to an altar
where I am once again to be sacrificed
to the laugh-a-minute God of Israel
and the wanton Muse of Poetry.

"I've never gone to Hebrew School," I protest.
He laughs, she cries.
"And I've never even been Bar Mitzvah'd."
He doubles over, if that were possible, which
of course it is. She is beside herself.

"And you know, I was only half circumcised
by a Gentile doctor who didn't know what he was doing!"

Now they both dissolve in laughter.

Ite missa est.

III. Something Like a Life

NEVER

We never.
I would have remembered. And I don't.
I remember standing on the beach.
That night. I remember how chilly it was.
But the rest you must have made up.
I wish it were all true. It would be something
like a life. Not a very good one but something.
Sand got in my shoes. I remember that.
I was just wearing what I thought I had to wear
at the office. This was before I lost the job? Or after.
I see green. I see someone dressed in green.
I think that's enough to recall.
Close the door behind you when you leave.

MY FATHER

I could not see him bait a hook.
Why would he do that even to a worm?
But he remained a happy member
of the "72" Fishing Club (its home,
the Austin Inn Bar and Grill, located on
72nd Avenue, Forest Hills)
as long as it lasted, with its annual change
of "commodore" recorded duly on a plaque on the barroom's wall.
He might not have ever baited a hook
but hanging out gregariously on a boat on whatever high sea
pouring down companionably the beer and the whiskey
was just one of his favorite voyages.
"We're only passing through, show a little strength,"
he'd often say to me. "At least I know I'm Jewish,"
my mother would throw at him whenever he pissed
her off, which was frequently. But so did he,
in his arch way. I never saw him bait a hook,
yet he might have; I was never there to see.

A MAN AND HIS CLONE

I am on a westbound train, sitting at a white tableclothed table
playing casino with my cloned son Robert.
Robert's not too bright, but he's goodhearted, or wants to be.
He is beating me more often than not at this game I've taught him,
which my father (of whom, unfortunately, I'm no clone) taught me.
I think we are in Oklahoma, or maybe New Mexico—one of those
gorgeous western states speeding past us as we play our cards.
I would ask Robert where we are, only I know he wouldn't know if I don't.
We are on our way to California, where a man and his clone may
feel reasonably secure. I once
had a premonition I would die there; that was in 1965. It
hardly matters now.

BOWERY, CIRCA 1950

The ogre that sits inside history
lays his head on the bar and dozes off.
The bartender comes over, pushes his
shoulder to wake him and
pours him another waterglass full of Five Star port.
The old monster tries to growl but only
coughs up a lunger for a lesson
which he aims at the nearest spittoon, but misses.
"There'll never be another moment like this
moment," he weeps. Nobody listens, so he
drains his glass and calls for another.

STEPPING STONE

The original wheel
with all its details
is the object of a profound study
conducted by scientists with fading straw hair
and misted spectacles.

I and a number of
friends and chance acquaintances
have been assigned the
task of washing the test tubes.
We are told this is quite
an honor and stepping stone
to even greater achievements.

I have a bird singing in my brain.
Or do I?

UP-RIVER

The day turned dung grey.
I felt like crying.
Then it began to rain
and I took a can of beer and
sat out on the porch and watched it.
For a while the way it came down
on all the overhanging weeds and
trees and whatnot reminded me
of one of Joseph Conrad's stories of
up-river God knows where, in the "Orient"
and there's me on my porch, my
veranda, with my can of
bloody Belgian controlled Budweiser,
and I thought, I am one lucky bloke
to be able to be out here on my
veranda watching my own personal
monsoon, and I didn't feel as much
like crying, and my cat scratched
at the door asking to join me, and
by God, I let him…

THE END OF THE SERIES

A scarecrow left his field
and hurried off to an open poetry reading.
It was the final one of a long series
and he didn't want to miss it.
When he took his hat off a lot of straw
fell at his feet. So he put his hat back on
and looked in vain for the sheet
of paper on which he scribbled his
wistful poem about crows and clouds.
He had to recite the whole thing from memory.
He managed to stammer through it
and the crowd applauded as if they really meant it.

MEDITATION

See there the umbilical knotting?
The universe?
The belly of the All?
I am sitting
listening to the breathing, the crooning.

ART-DECO BLUES

There they are—Nick and Nora
aboard the Twentieth Century Limited
a spread of caviar and Champagne between them.
They are my mother and father
before I came along to blow their cool—
Nick and Nora,
Abe and Mary—

I am sorry.
I am so fucking
sorry.

THE QUESTION

Kafka! Oh Franz, wait up a bit...
I thought I saw his ears perk up
but he walked on even faster.
Oh Franz do stop a moment I have
something to ask you...
but he just walked on.
I am I guess you could almost call
lame...even with the help of my walking
stick, I had no hope of overtaking him...
Kafka! Franz! please wait...

THE MUDDLE

The world being in the muddle it is
isn't it time for the chthonic spirits
the "Old Ones" to arise from the demonic depths
to reassert their ancient dominion?
Of course, we now have Buffy the Vampire
Slayer, a nice Jewish girl with a
cross around her neck
to fight the monsters to the death;
but even more reassuring,
we have the corporate elites,
wonderfully resilient, who are capable
of matching evil for evil with the monsters
and even making deals behind poor
Buffy's liberal back!

BRAGGING RIGHTS

You know,
I never wanted to
like, have a lot of money.
Rich people have all these
stresses and strains.
They own too many things and
have to pay people to keep track.
And even when they're vacationing
they're working.
They're always competing, never
satisfied, and they have to deal with all
these experts: lawyers, brokers, surgeons,
hit men. I just never wanted that.
I guess I didn't have to go as far as I did
to avoid it, but
hell, it's my only success!

HBO SPECIAL

You know the house next door to me
that's been vacant for years
'cause they wanted too much money for it?
It's been sold.
My new neighbors,
the Sopranos,
move in tomorrow.
I guess they'll want me
to do something about my lawn.

CAREER

My cache of stolen court jewels
is somewhere in this
accursed house.
I will find them.
There is this goofy couple sent by
the director to interfere with my designs
but I will thwart them.
This is my
final film and my
last chance to star.

BEEFSTEW, TOO

for Gomer Rees

There's that erect old veteran, eyes glittering,
not looking half my age, let alone his own 93;
he's chatting away with someone. Everyone's chatting
with someone.
But not me. I'm chatting with no one and nobody's
chatting with me. A poet I used to know in the city
wrote a poem about such a scene, and now I come
to a belated appreciation of that poem.

I don't know why I should repeat it. But I do.

I move my psyche around the room
searching vainly for another theme
but don't find any. This will have to do.

After coming home alone in the cold
and dining on some very unappetizing beef stew, too.

MY LATEST HOBBY

My latest hobby is collecting videos
of old films: VCR's; no DVD's.
Ghosts appear prominently in my latest acquisitions;
Ingmar Bergman's next to last film, "Fanny and Alexander"
for one, Nicole Kidman's stunning performance in
"The Others" for another. Is this
a sign from the world of ghosts
that I may soon see one, or be one?
In Chile, at this very moment,
they are bringing up the buried miners,
from what could have been their grave.
So many grateful Lazarus's.

LAMENT OF A LESSER PRIMATE

I'm at the edge of the jungle
where my friends used to live.
I loiter here, why, I don't really know.
They won't be back. And if they
really were my friends,
they wouldn't have gone.
I am the only one in this
whole country like me.
There are a lot of them that look
like me, but they just aren't
like me. The ones that left
I guess weren't like me either.
They didn't even look like me,
come to think of it. Oh God!

THIS BIG WINDOW

I have this big window.
What I need is a telescope to peer into the
night sky with
to look for moons or comets or
astrally projected floaters
or maybe see who's
undressing in the window
across the road...
The heavens are overgrown,
it seems to me, like my
seriously neglected yard,
like my sluggish imagination,
like my boxloads of books and neuroses.

The New York Quarterly Foundation, Inc.
New York, New York

Poetry Magazine
Since 1969

Edgy, fresh, groundbreaking, eclectic—voices from all walks of life.

Definitely NOT your mama's poetry magazine!

The *New York Quarterly* has been defining the term contemporary American poetry since its first craft interview with W. H. Auden.

Interviews • Essays • and of course, lots of poems.

www.nyquarterly.org

No contest! That's correct, NYQ Books are NO CONTEST to other small presses because we do not support ourselves through contests. Our books are carefully selected by invitation only, so you know that NYQ Books are produced with the same editorial integrity as the magazine that has brought you the most eclectic contemporary American poetry since 1969.

Books

nyqbooks.org

poetry at the edge™

www.ingramcontent.com/pod-product-compliance
Lightning Source LLC
LaVergne TN
LVHW041340080426
835512LV00006B/553